MIND BENDERS® B3

DEDUCTIVE THINKING SKILLS

D0775296

SERIES TITLES
Mind Benders® Beginning Book 1
Mind Benders® Beginning Book 2
Mind Benders® Warm Up
Mind Benders® A1
Mind Benders® A2
Mind Benders® A3
Mind Benders® A4
Mind Benders® B1
Mind Benders® B2
Mind Benders® B3
Mind Benders® B4
Mind Benders® C1
Mind Benders® C2
Mind Benders® C3

ANITA HARNADEK

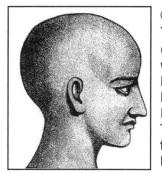

© 2005, 2000, 1981
THE CRITICAL THINKING CO.
(BRIGHT MINDS™)
www.CriticalThinking.com
P.O. Box 1610 • Seaside • CA 93955-1610
Phone 800-458-4849 • FAX 831-393-3277
ISBN 0-89455-125-6
The individual purchaser of this book is licensed to reproduce
the student pages for use within one home or one classroom.
Printed in the United States of America

TABLE OF CONTENTS

© 2005 The Critical Thinking Co. • www.CriticalThinking.com • 800-458-4849

TEACHER SUGGESTIONS

PURPOSE

Students with wide ranges of ability, motivation, and achievement seem to be remarkably attracted to Mind Benders® problems. Students think Mind Benders® are fun, not work. The purpose of the MIND BENDERS® series is to improve deductive reasoning, reading comprehension skills, and organized analysis skills.

GENERAL INFORMATION

There are fourteen exercise books in this series:

MIND BENDERS® Beginning BOOK 1

MIND BENDERS® Beginning BOOK 2

MIND BENDERS® Warm-Up

MIND BENDERS® A1

MIND BENDERS® A2

MIND BENDERS® A3

MIND BENDERS® A4

MIND BENDERS® B1

MIND BENDERS® B2

MIND BENDERS® B3

MIND BENDERS® B4

MIND BENDERS® C1

MIND BENDERS® C2

MIND BENDERS® C3

The **A** series is easy, **C** is difficult, and **B** is, clearly, in-between with medium level problems.

The Beginning level is the easiest level and is often used to introduce students (as young as preschool) to Mind Benders® problems and charts. MIND BENDERS® WARM UP (see listing of titles above) has easy problems with a handful of medium problems. This book is used to give auditory Mind Benders® to students.

Since some teachers will need more problems for their students than others, more than one book is available in each of the A, B, and C levels. Within a level, there is no substantial difference in difficulty between the books offered. (For example, a teacher who needs 15 problems at the "A" level may order any of the four MIND

BENDERS® books in the A series.)

See page iv for general comments about assumptions that can be made from clues.

HELPFUL HINTS ABOUT SOLVING MIND BENDERS®

Most Mind Benders® in the Beginning, A, B, and C categories are solved more easily if a chart is used than if the solver simply makes notes about the clues given. To help students solve the problems, each Mind Bender® is accompanied by a chart made especially for that particular problem.

See page vi for a step-by-step explanation of how to use charts to solve Mind Benders® problems, including the way each chart looks after each step. None of the problems used there are used as exercises in any of the MIND BENDERS® books.

The instructions (in highly abbreviated form, of course) are these: To fill in a chart, make a notation in each square which is eliminated by a clue. (The notation might be the clue number or the word "no," for example.) When there is only one blank square left in a row (or column) within a category, then "X" that square. Then note the elimination of all the other squares in the matching column and row. When a chart contains three or more categories, then either the elimination of a square or the "X"ing of a square may also give you more information about previous clues. (For example, if you know that Mr. Brown owns the red car and you have just discovered that the Chevrolet is not the red car, then you have also discovered that Mr. Brown does not own the Chevrolet.)

SOLUTIONS

Note 1: Each problem has only one solution. If the notation used for eliminations is simply a "no," then the completed chart will have an "X" for each combination named in the solutions given below, and the chart will have a "no" everywhere else. If the notation used for elimination is a clue number, however, then the completed chart may vary from one student to another. (This is because eliminations can sometimes be made in different orders.)

© 2005 The Critical Thinking Co. • www.CriticalThinking.com • 800-458-4849

Note 2: If your solutions do not agree with those given, refer to the Examples and Step-by-Step Procedures on page vii for information on how to use charts to solve Mind Benders® problems.

ABOUT THE CLUES IN MIND BENDERS®

In general, the MIND BENDERS® assume that you will, when using the clues, apply three guidelines unless a problem leads you to believe otherwise:

1. Think of everyday situations rather than of highly unusual exceptions.

2. Think of standards which are generally acceptable to U.S. society as a whole.

3. Use common sense and context in deciding what the clues mean.

Following are examples:

a. Assume that only males have male names (John, Robert, Dave) and only females have female names (Mary, Jennifer, Cathy), but be careful not to make such assumptions about unisex names (Pat, Chris).

b. Assume that typical U.S. social relationships apply. For example, if John is engaged to Mary, you may assume that they know each other. You may assume that very close relatives know each other.

c. Don't assume that rare age relationships may apply. For example, don't assume that a 7 year old might be a college graduate, or that a parent might be younger than his or her adopted child. On the other hand, although most cases of age may be in one direction, enough cases in the other direction may exist so that these would not be considered especially unusual. For example, a husband may be a good deal younger than his wife, or a 45 year old may get the mumps.

d. Assume that animals are of normal size. For example, "a horse" is not "a pygmy horse"; "a small dog" is smaller than a goat; a "large dog"

is simply one of the larger breeds of dogs. If a problem talks about a cat and a fox, assume that the cat is smaller than the fox. Do not think that maybe the cat is fully grown and the fox is a few weeks old.

e. Assume that animals are called by their usual names within the context. For example, if John and Mary have a pet dog and a pet cat, assume that the cat is an ordinary household cat, rather than maybe a tiger or a leopard.

f. Don't look for tricky situations. For example, suppose that the problem has four houses in a row (and no other houses), and suppose that Debby lives next door to Gary. Don't assume that Debby or Gary might live in a garage between two of the houses. That is, assume that they live in two of the four houses in the problem.

g. Assume that typical U.S. social situations apply. For example, if John went on a date with Abbott, assume two things: (1) Abbott is a female; (2) neither John nor Abbott is married, since (a) when a married couple goes out, we do not call it a "date," and (b) if either one is married to someone else, then it is not typical for him or her to be dating someone.

h. Pay attention to what the clues say. For example, suppose that a problem has four people, and suppose that one clue says, "Cathy and the dentist ride to work together in a car pool." Also suppose that another clue says, "Brown, who does not know any of the other three people, is not the typist." Then you should deduce that neither Cathy nor the dentist is Brown.

i. Exact wording to eliminate ambiguities sometimes makes a clue too long. The clue is then shortened to the point where it is unambiguous to most people, but some people would still recognize ambiguities and object to the wording. In such cases, consider the context and the intent of the clue. As examples:

(1) "Neither Bob nor Young lives in the white house," means, "Bob is not Young, and Bob does not live in the white house, and Young

          © 2005 The Critical Thinking Co. • www.CriticalThinking.com • 800-458-4849

does not live in the white house."

(2) "John and Abbott went bowling with Dave and Smith," means, "Four different people went bowling together. One of these was John, one was Abbott, one was Dave, and one was Smith."

(3) "Jane doesn't know either Mary or the artist," means, "Jane doesn't know Mary, and Jane doesn't know the artist, and Mary is not the artist."

(4) "Neither Carol nor Bill went to the party, and Norris didn't go, either," refers to three different people.

(5) In general, "neither ... nor" and "either ... or" sentences will refer to separate things, as in the above examples. Just plain "or" sentences, however, are sometimes less definite, as in this example: "Neither Becky nor Jackson has the dog or is the secretary." Here, Becky and Jackson are different people, but we aren't sure that the person who has the dog is not also the secretary.

© 2005 The Critical Thinking Co. • www.CriticalThinking.com • 800-458-4849

EXAMPLES AND STEP-BY-STEP PROCEDURES

A Mind Bender® problem gives you two or more lists of things and asks you to match each item in one list with an item in the other list. Finding answers is easier if a chart is made showing all the lists at once and is then filled in. Note that the number of small boxes (within one large box) is the square of the number of things in any one list. (Example 1 has three things in each list, so each large box has 9 small boxes).

THREE-DIMENSIONAL PROBLEMS

To solve a three-dimensional problem, we make the chart so that each item in each list can be compared with each item in both other lists.

EXAMPLE 1

Problem: Davis, Edwards, and Farman are an astronaut, a bookbinder, and a skin diver. Their ages are 25, 30, and 35. Match each person's name, job, and age.

1. Davis is younger than the astronaut but older than Farman.

2. The skin diver is younger than the bookbinder.

   Solution: To help keep our thinking straight on clue 1, we'll write in mathematical symbols: F < D < A. Then Farman is the youngest, Davis is in the middle, and the astronaut is the oldest. So Farman is 25, Davis is 30, and the astronaut is 35.

   It is important to notice here that if the puzzle involved four people instead of three, we could not say that Farman is the youngest or that the astronaut is the oldest. The most we could say is (1) Farman is not either of the two oldest people, (2) Davis is not either the oldest or the youngest person, and (3) the astronaut is not either of the two youngest people. Let's look at how the chart works for this kind of problem.

Clue 1, step 1

	A	B	SD	25	30	35
D	1				X	
E						
F	1			X		
25						
30						
35	X					

Clue 1, step 2

	A	B	SD	25	30	35
D	1			25	X	D
E				25	30	
F	1			X	F	F
25	A					
30	A					
35	X	35	35			

Clue 1, step 3

	A	B	SD	25	30	35
D	1			25	X	D
E	X	E	E	25	30	X
F	1			X	F	F
25	A					
30	A					
35	X	35	35			

© 2005 The Critical Thinking Co. • www.CriticalThinking.com • 800-458-4849

Clue 2 says the skin diver is younger than the bookbinder. The chart (from clue 1, step 3) says that Edwards, the astronaut, is 35. This leaves ages 25 and 30. So the skin diver is 25 and the bookbinder is 30. But we know from the chart that Farman is 25 and Davis is 30. So Farman is the skin diver and Davis is the bookbinder.

	A	B	SD	25	30	35
D	1	X	SD	25	X	D
E	X	E	E	25	30	X
F	1	F	X	X	F	F
25	A	25	X			
30	A	X	SD			
35	X	35	35			

Solution: Davis, bookbinder, 30; Edwards, astronaut, 35; Farman, skin diver, 25.

EXAMPLE 2

Problem: Davis, Edwards, Farman, and Gurley are an astronaut, a bookbinder, a plumber, and a skin diver. Their first names are Harold, Jenny, Ken, and Laura. Match up each person's full name and job.

1. Farman and the astronaut joined the same fraternity in college.

2. Edwards said she'd teach Jenny how to swim.

3. Ken asked the plumber if he could install a solar heating system for him.

4. Davis enjoys her work.

Solution: (Can you solve this one before reading the solution below?)

Clue 1　　　　　　　　　　　Clue 2　　　　　　　　　　　Clue 3, step 1

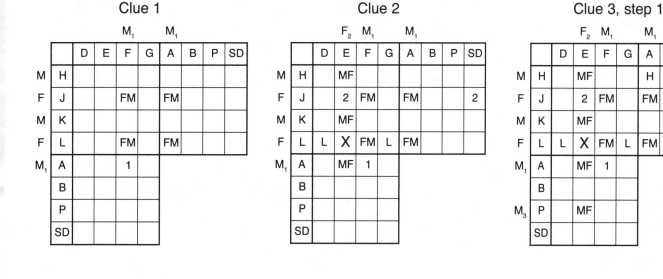

© 2005 The Critical Thinking Co. • www.CriticalThinking.com • 800-458-4849

Clue 3, step 2

		F₂	M₁		M₁	M₃		
		D	E	F	G	A	B	P	SD
M	H			MF		H	H	X	H
F	J		2	FM		FM		FM	2
M	K			MF		X	K	3	K
F	L	L		X	FM	L	FM		FM
M₁	A			MF	1				
	B								
M₃	P			MF					
	SD								

Clue 3, step 3*

		F₂	M₁		M₁	M₃		
		D	E	F	G	A	B	P	SD
M	H			MF		H	H	X	H
F	J		2	FM		FM		FM	2
M	K			MF	3,1*	X	K	3	K
F	L	L		X	FM	L	FM		FM
M₁	A			MF	1				
	B								
M₃	P			MF					
	SD								

*The "F" column says Farman is not the astronaut (clue 1). But step 2 of clue 3 says Ken is the astronaut. Therefore, Ken is not Farman.

Clue 3, step 4

		F₂	M₁		M₁	M₃		
		D	E	F	G	A	B	P	SD
M	H			MF		H	H	X	H
F	J		2	FM		FM	X	FM	2
M	K			MF	3,1	X	K	3	K
F	L	L		X	FM	L	FM	B	FM	X
M₁	A			MF	1				
	B								
M₃	P			MF					
	SD								

Clue 3, step 5

		F₂	M₁		M₁	M₃		
		D	E	F	G	A	B	P	SD
M	H	H		MF	X	H	H	H	X	H
F	J		2	FM		FM	X	FM	2
M	K			MF	3,1	X	K	3	K
F	L	L		X	FM	L	FM	B	FM	X
M₁	A			MF	1				
	B								
M₃	P			MF					
	SD								

Clue 3, step 6

		F₂	M₁		M₁	M₃		
		D	E	F	G	A	B	P	SD
M	H	H		MF	X	H	H	H	X	H
F	J		2	FM		FM	X	FM	2
M	K			MF	3,1	X	K	3	K
F	L	L		X	FM	L	FM	B	FM	X
M₁	A			MF	1				
	B					F			
M₃	P	P		MF	X	P			
	SD					F			

Clue 3, step 7

		F₂	M₁		M₁	M₃		
		D	E	F	G	A	B	P	SD
M	H	H		MF	X	H	H	H	X	H
F	J		2	FM		FM	X	FM	2
M	K			MF	3,1	X	K	3	K
F	L	L		X	FM	L	FM	B	FM	X
M₁	A			MF	1				
	B			E	F				
M₃	P	P		MF	X	P			
	SD	SD		X	F	SD			

Clue 4, step 1

		F₄	F₂	M₁		M₁	M₃	
		D	E	F	G	A	B	P	SD
M	H	H		MF	X	H	H	H	X	H
F	J	X	2	FM	J	FM	X	FM	2
M	K	MF		MF	3,1	X	K	3	K
F	L	L		X	FM	L	FM	B	FM	X
M₁	A			MF	1				
	B			E	F				
M₃	P	P		MF	X	P			
	SD	SD	SD	X	F	SD			

Clue 4, step 2

		F₄	F₂	M₁		M₁	M₃	
		D	E	F	G	A	B	P	SD
M	H	H		MF	X	H	H	H	X	H
F	J	X	2	FM	J	FM	X	FM	2
M	K	MF		MF	3,1	X	K	3	K
F	L	L		X	FM	L	FM	B	FM	X
M₁	A	D		MF	1				
	B	X		E	F	B			
M₃	P	P		MF	X	P			
	SD	SD	SD	X	F	SD			

Clue 4, step 3

		F₄	F₂	M₁		M₁	M₃	
		D	E	F	G	A	B	P	SD
M	H	H		MF	X	H	H	H	X	H
F	J	X	2	FM	J	FM	X	FM	2
M	K	MF		MF	3,1	X	X	K	3	K
F	L	L		X	FM	L	FM	B	FM	X
M₁	A	D		MF	1	X			
	B	X		E	F	B			
M₃	P	P		MF	X	P			
	SD	SD	SD	X	F	SD			

The solution is this: Harold Farman, plumber; Jenny Davis, bookbinder; Ken Gurley, astronaut; Laura Edwards, skin diver.

© 2005 The Critical Thinking Co. • www.CriticalThinking.com • 800-458-4849

Here's one more three-dimensional puzzle for you to try before we go on to a four-dimensional puzzle.

EXAMPLE 3

Problem: Harold, Jenny, Ken, and Laura are 12, 16, 20, and 25 years old. Their last names are Davis, Edwards, Farman, and Gurley. Find each person's full name and age.

1. Harold's and Gurley's ages are perfect squares.

2. Edwards is Jenny's older sister.

3. Farman is younger than Ken but older than Edwards' sister.

Solution: Clue 1: (a) Harold is not Gurley. (b) The only perfect squares listed are 16 and 25, so neither Harold nor Gurley is 12 or 20.

Clue 1

		D	E	F	G	12	16	20	25
M	H			1	1			1	
F	J								
M	K								
F	L								
	12			1					
	16								
	20			1					
	25								

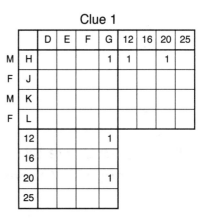

Clue 2, step 1: (a) Edwards is a female and is not Jenny. So Edwards is Laura. (b) From clue 1, the ages of 16 and 25 are taken by Ken and Gurley, and Laura Edwards is neither of these people. So she is either 12 or 20. But she is older than Jenny, so she cannot be the youngest person, 12. So Laura Edwards is 20.

Clue 2, step 1

			F₂					F₂	
		D	E	F	G	12	16	20	25
M	H		MF		1	1		1	
F	J		2					20	
M	K		MF					20	
F	L	L	X	L	L	2	2,1	X	2,1
	12		2		1				
	16		2,1						
F₂	20	20	X	20	1				
	25		2,1						

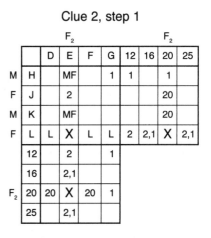

Clue 2, step 2: (a) Laura Edwards is 20 and is older than Jenny, so Jenny is either 12 or 16. (b) So neither Jenny nor Laura is 25. Then the 25-year-old is a male.

Clue 2, step 2

			F₂					F₂	M₂
		D	E	F	G	12	16	20	25
M	H		MF		1	1		1	
F	J		2					20	2
M	K		MF					20	
F	L	L	X	L	L	2	2,1	X	2,1
	12		2		1				
	16		2,1						
F₂	20	20	X	20	1				
M₂	25		2,1						

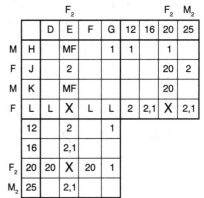

© 2005 The Critical Thinking Co. • www.CriticalThinking.com • 800-458-4849

Clue 3, step 1: Edwards' sister is Jenny (clue 2), so Farman is younger than Ken but older than Jenny. In mathematical notation, J < F < K. Laura Edwards, 20, is not Jenny or Farman or Ken, so the only ages left are 12, 16 and 25. So Jenny is 12, Farman is 16, and Ken is 25.

Clue 3, step 1

		D	E	F	G	12	16	20	25
			F_2					F_2	M_2
M	H		MF		1	1		1	25
F	J		2			X	J	20	2
M	K		MF			12	K	20	X
F	L	L	X	L	L	2	2,1	X	2,1
	12		2	F	1				
	16	16	2,1	X	16				
F_2	20	20	X	20	1				
M_2	25		2,1	F					

Clue 3, step 2: We look for remaining spaces we are forced to X, and we X them.

Clue 3, step 2

		D	E	F	G	12	16	20	25
			F_2					F_2	M_2
M	H		MF		1	1	X	1	25
F	J		2			X	J	20	2
M	K		MF			12	K	20	X
F	L	L	X	L	L	2	2,1	X	2,1
	12	X	2	F	1				
	16	16	2,1	X	16				
F_2	20	20	X	20	1				
M_2	25	D	2,1	F	X				

Clue 3, step 3: (a) The chart shows that Harold and Farman are both 16, so Harold is Farman. (b) Jenny and Davis are both 12, so Jenny is Davis. (c) Only the K/G space is left. Since Ken and Gurley are both 25, we X this space.

Clue 3, step 3

		D	E	F	G	12	16	20	25
			F_2					F_2	M_2
M	H	H	MF	X	1	1	X	1	25
F	J	X	2	F	J	X	J	20	2
M	K	D	MF	F	X	12	K	20	X
F	L	L	X	L	L	2	2,1	X	2,1
	12	X	2	F	1				
	16	16	2,1	X	16				
F_2	20	20	X	20	1				
M_2	25	D	2,1	F	X				

So the solution is this: Harold Farman, 16; Jenny Davis, 12; Ken Gurley, 25; Laura Edwards, 20.

© 2005 The Critical Thinking Co. • www.CriticalThinking.com • 800-458-4849

FOUR- AND FIVE-DIMENSIONAL PROBLEMS

A problem of four or more dimensions is solved the same way as the others. Again, the chart must be made so that each list can be compared with all the other lists.

EXAMPLE 4

Problem: Davis, Edwards, and Gurley are the first, second, and third basemen for the Detroit Tigers. Their first names are Harold, José, and Ken. Their ages are 23, 25, and 28. From the clues below, match up everything.

1. The second baseman has a higher batting average than Ken or Davis.

2. The first baseman is younger than Edwards and older than Ken.

3. José and Davis ate pizza with some of the rest of the team after yesterday's game.

Solution:

Clue 1

Clue 2, step 1

(K < 1ˢᵗ < E)

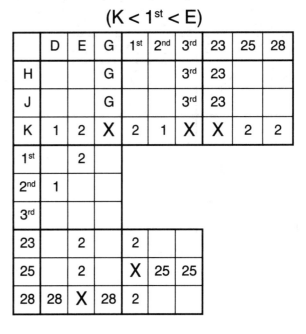

Clue 1

	D	E	G	1st	2nd	3rd	23	25	28
H									
J									
K	1			1					
1st						
2nd	1					
3rd						
23						
25						
28						

Clue 2, step 1 (K < 1ˢᵗ < E)

	D	E	G	1st	2nd	3rd	23	25	28
H			G			3rd	23		
J			G			3rd	23		
K	1	2	X	2	1	X	X	2	2
1st		2				
2nd	1					
3rd						
23		2		2		
25		2		X	25	25
28	28	X		28	2	

© 2005 The Critical Thinking Co. • www.CriticalThinking.com • 800-458-4849

Clue 2, step 2 (Gurley is Ken, so post facts about Ken in Gurley's column. Also match "3rd" and "23.")

	D	E	G	1st	2nd	3rd	23	25	28
H			G			3rd	23		
J			G			3rd	23		
K	1	2	X	2	1	X	X	2	2
1st		2	K						
2nd	1		K						
3rd	3rd	3rd	X						
23	23	2	X	2	23	X			
25		2	K	X	25	25			
28	28	X	28	2		3rd			

Clue 2, step 3

	D	E	G	1st	2nd	3rd	23	25	28
H			G			3rd	23		
J			G			3rd	23		
K	1	2	X	2	1	X	X	2	2
1st	X	2	K						
2nd	1	X	K						
3rd	3rd	3rd	X						
23	23	2	X	2	23	X			
25	X	2	K	X	25	25			
28	28	X	28	2	X	3rd			

Clue 3, step 1

	D	E	G	1st	2nd	3rd	23	25	28
H	X	H	G			3rd	23		
J	3	X	G			3rd	23		
K	1	2	X	2	1	X	X	2	2
1st	X	2	K						
2nd	1	X	K						
3rd	3rd	3rd	X						
23	23	2	X	2	23	X			
25	X	2	K	X	25	25			
28	28	X	28	2	X	3rd			

The rest of the entries are now forced, so the chart is left for you to complete.

The solution is this: Harold Davis, first baseman, 25; José Edwards, second baseman, 28; Ken Gurley, third baseman, 23.

                          © 2005 The Critical Thinking Co. • www.CriticalThinking.com • 800-458-4849

The problem above gave us four lists of things to match up (first names, last names, positions, and ages), and so is called a four-dimensional problem. A general chart for a four-dimensional problem would look like the one at the right.

	headings for second list	headings for third list	headings for fourth list
headings for first list	small boxes	small boxes	small boxes
headings for third list	small boxes		
headings for fourth list	small boxes	small boxes	

A general chart for a five-dimensional problem (a problem with five lists of things to match up) would look like the one at the right.

	headings for second list	headings for third list	headings for fourth list	headings for fifth list
headings for first list	small boxes	small boxes	small boxes	small boxes
headings for third list	small boxes			
headings for fourth list	small boxes	small boxes		
headings for fifth list	small boxes	small boxes	small boxes	

© 2005 The Critical Thinking Co. • www.CriticalThinking.com • 800-458-4849

1. Playground Games

Charles, Edward, Irene, José, and Patricia, whose last names are Bingman, Darby, Frye, Morgan, and Wilson, each have a favorite game (hide and seek, red rover, red light, Simon says, and tag).

Read the clues below and match up everything.

1. The boy whose favorite game is "hide and seek" is a year younger than Darby.

2. Patricia likes to play "red rover" almost as much as she likes to play her favorite game.

3. Morgan invited José and Frye to her birthday party.

4. Charles and the boy whose favorite game is "red light" got in trouble in school yesterday, and it didn't help their moods any when Frye teased them both about it.

5. Wilson, who doesn't like running games, sometimes walks to school with two of her friends, Charles and Bingman.

© 2005 The Critical Thinking Co. • www.CriticalThinking.com • 800-458-4849

Chart for Problem 1

	Bingman	Darby	Frye	Morgan	Wilson	hide and seek	red rover	red light	Simon says	tag
Charles										
Edward										
Irene										
José										
Patricia										
hide and seek										
red rover										
red light										
Simon says										
tag										

© 2005 The Critical Thinking Co. • www.CriticalThinking.com • 800-458-4849

2. Ice Cream

Elmer, Frank, Michelle, Nerissa, and Zora, whose last names are Anderson, Dowden, Garvey, Hinton, and Jones, have favorite ice cream flavors, one to each person. The flavors are butter pecan, chocolate, lemon, strawberry, and vanilla.

Match everything up from the clues below.

1 . Jones and the person whose favorite is butter pecan bought Hinton his favorite ice cream.

2. Anderson and his sister both have the same favorite, which isn't chocolate.

3. Michelle, Garvey, and the girl whose favorite is butter pecan went to the ice cream store with Elmer and Anderson.

4. The girl whose favorite is lemon teased Michelle about having ice cream on her nose.

5. Anderson and the person whose favorite is strawberry walked to the store with Michelle.

6. Zora's favorite is not butter pecan, but she likes it a lot anyway.

© 2005 The Critical Thinking Co. • www.CriticalThinking.com • 800-458-4849

Chart for Problem 2

	Anderson	Dowden	Garvey	Hinton	Jones	butter pecan	chocolate	lemon	strawberry	vanilla
Elmer										
Frank										
Michelle										
Nerissa										
Zora										
butter pecan										
chocolate										
lemon										
strawberry										
vanilla										

3.   Pet Cats

Abner, Crystal, Edmund, and Joy, whose last names are Dinton, Harmon, Landon, and Magland, each have a cat. The colors of the cats are black, gray, white, and yellow, and the cats' names are Fluffy, Kitty, Pretty, and Sleepy.

From the clues below, match up everything.

1.   Magland has the yellow cat.

2.   Sleepy's owner, who is neither Joy nor Harmon, does not have the gray cat.

3.   Abner's and Landon's cats are short-haired, while Crystal's and Dinton's cats are long-haired.

4.   Neither Pretty nor the gray cat, which are short-haired, is owned by Edmund.

5.   Crystal's cat, which is not white or yellow, is not Fluffy.

© 2005 The Critical Thinking Co. • www.CriticalThinking.com • 800-458-4849

Chart for Problem 3

	Dinton	Harmon	Landon	Magland	black	gray	white	yellow	Fluffy	Kitty	Pretty	Sleepy
Abner												
Crystal												
Edmund												
Joy												
black												
gray												
white												
yellow												
Fluffy												
Kitty												
Pretty												
Sleepy												

© 2005 The Critical Thinking Co. • www.CriticalThinking.com • 800-458-4849

4. Catching a Cold

Caroline, Dominic, Edna, Gary, Helmut, and Inez, whose last names are Kaufman, Newton, O'Brien, Reisner, Wyndham, and Zaharias, each caught a cold from someone in the family (aunt, brother, father, mother, sister, and uncle).

Match up everything from the clues below.

1. Caroline's cold lasted longer than Wyndham's.

2. Reisner didn't catch his cold from his sister, and neither did Helmut.

3. Kaufman and O'Brien caught their colds from females.

4. Edna didn't catch her cold from her father or an uncle.

5. O'Brien's mother didn't have a cold, and neither did Gary's.

6. Caroline doesn't have an uncle, and neither does Zaharias.

7. Neither Dominic's nor O'Brien's cold lasted long.

8. Males caught their colds from females.

© 2005 The Critical Thinking Co. • www.CriticalThinking.com • 800-458-4849

Chart for Problem 4

	Kaufman	Newton	O'Brien	Reisner	Wyndham	Zaharias	aunt	brother	father	mother	sister	uncle
Caroline												
Dominic												
Edna												
Gary												
Helmut												
Inez												
aunt												
brother												
father												
mother												
sister												
uncle												

© 2005 The Critical Thinking Co. • www.CriticalThinking.com • 800-458-4849

5. Keeping Cool

One very hot Saturday afternoon, Ada, George, Joanne, Myrtle, and Nehemiah, whose last names are Cranbrook, Emmerson, Ipson, Kribb, and Larson, found different ways to keep cool. One stayed in the basement at home, one went shopping in an air-conditioned department store, one sat in front of a fan, one sat under a hose spray in the back yard at home, and one went swimming at a public beach.

From the clues below, match up everything. Assume that all clues refer to that particular afternoon.

1. Ipson telephoned Joanne, who had to work in an office downtown all afternoon, to see how she was doing.

2. Neither Ada nor Emmerson got wet.

3. Neither Ipson nor Larson stayed home.

4. The person who sat under the hose spray, who is not Kribb, got sunburned when he fell asleep for an hour.

5. George didn't go swimming, and neither did Myrtle.

6. Kribb did not spend the afternoon in a basement or a department store.

7. Ada does not know Larson.

© 2005 The Critical Thinking Co. • www.CriticalThinking.com • 800-458-4849

Chart for Problem 5

	Cran-brook	Emmer-son	Ipson	Kribb	Larson	base-ment	depart-ment store	fan	hose	swimming
Ada										
George										
Joanne										
Myrtle										
Nehe-miah										
base-ment										
depart-ment store										
fan										
hose										
swimming										

6. Bread and Marmalade

Amelia, Bernard, Derick, and Eula May, whose last names are Grader, Horton, Ingles, and Johnstone, each had a piece of bread (French bread, pumpernickel, rye, and whole wheat) with marmalade (cherry, orange, raspberry, and strawberry) on it.

Match up everything from the clues below.

1. Derick, who is not the oldest, is older than Ingles.

2. Johnstone is younger than the person who had orange marmalade and older than the person who had whole wheat bread.

3. Horton, a male, is not Bernard.

4. Amelia is older than the person who had cherry marmalade, who is older than the person who had pumpernickel bread.

5. Amelia didn't have French bread or orange marmalade.

6. Bernard, who is the youngest, did not have strawberry marmalade.

7. Eula May is not Johnstone.

© 2005 The Critical Thinking Co. • www.CriticalThinking.com • 800-458-4849

Chart for Problem 6

	Grader	Horton	Ingles	Johnstone	French bread	pumper-nickel	rye	whole wheat	cherry	orange	raspberry	strawberry
Amelia												
Bernard												
Derick												
Eula May												
French bread												
pumper-nickel												
rye												
whole wheat												
cherry												
orange												
raspberry												
strawberry												

© 2005 The Critical Thinking Co. • www.CriticalThinking.com • 800-458-4849

7. Show and Tell Pets

Allan, Daphne, Eunice, and Howard, whose last names are Franklin, Jackson, Kingsley, and Lohmer, created quite a stir when they took their pets (buffalo, cheetah, vulture, and zebra) to school for "Show and Tell." The colors of the pets' collars are green, red, white, and yellow.

Match up everything from the clues below.

1. The buffalo has a yellow collar.

2. Howard's pet does not have a green collar.

3. Neither Eunice's pet nor Franklin's pet flies or has a green collar.

4. Neither Daphne's nor Kingsley's pet has feathers or is spotted.

5. Neither Allan's pet nor the pet with the red collar has a beak.

6. The striped animal, which is the pet of neither Eunice nor Jackson, doesn't have a red collar.

© 2005 The Critical Thinking Co. • www.CriticalThinking.com • 800-458-4849

Chart for Problem 7

	Franklin	Jackson	Kingsley	Lohmer	buffalo	cheetah	vulture	zebra	green	red	white	yellow
Allan												
Daphne												
Eunice												
Howard												
buffalo												
cheetah												
vulture												
zebra												
green												
red												
white												
yellow												

8. How It Looks on Paper

Grady, Nelson, Ralston, and Tyler, whose first names are Adam, Deborah, Joan, and Vladimir, are four business people who ordered (and got) items printed (circulars, invoices, purchase orders, and stationery) in different typefaces (Futura, Helios, Korinna, and Oracle) and different type styles (bold, extra bold, light, and medium).

Read the clues below and match up everything.

1. The person who ordered the invoices, who didn't order Helios typeface or medium type style, and Adam and Tyler all asked Ralston how many items she ordered.

2. Nelson, who didn't order Korinna or Futura typeface, told Deborah that she was pleased with the type style, which wasn't light or extra bold.

3. The circulars, which were not printed in extra bold type style, were not ordered by Grady or Ralston.

4. The person who ordered Futura typeface ordered neither the light nor the extra bold type style, and she did not have stationery printed.

5. The items printed in Helios typeface were not printed in extra bold type.

© 2005 The Critical Thinking Co. • www.CriticalThinking.com • 800-458-4849

Chart for Problem 8

	Grady	Nelson	Ralston	Tyler	Futura	Helios	Korinna	Oracle	bold	extra bold	light	medium	circulars	invoices	purchase orders	stationery
Adam																
Deborah																
Joan																
Vladimir																
Futura																
Helios																
Korinna																
Oracle																
bold																
extra bold																
light																
medium																
circulars																
invoices																
purchase orders																
stationery																

9. Where They Work

Match the first name (Arthur, Bartholemew, Deborah, Edith, Francesca, and Gordon), the last name (Jankowski, Keyser, O'Rourke, Stoker, Tyler, and Werner), and the occupation (cosmetologist, hair stylist, labor arbitrator, mortician, pathologist, and union organizer) of each person.

1. Keyser does most of her work in a laboratory.

2. Stoker, who is not the hair stylist, has to know how to style hair.

3. O'Rourke gave Arthur some tips on how to do a better job.

4. Part of Bartholemew's job includes doing what Werner does on her job.

5. Edith and Tyler were bridesmaids, and Arthur and Jankowski were ushers, at the cosmetologist's wedding last week.

6. Gordon is not O'Rourke.

7. Francesca is not the pathologist or the union organizer, and neither is Edith.

© 2005 The Critical Thinking Co. • www.CriticalThinking.com • 800-458-4849

Chart for Problem 9

	Jankowski	Keyser	O'Rourke	Stoker	Tyler	Werner	cosmetol-ogist	hair stylist	labor arbitrator	mortician	pathol-ogist	union organizer
Arthur												
Bartho-lemew												
Deborah												
Edith												
Francesca												
Gordon												
cosmetol-ogist												
hair stylist												
labor arbitrator												
mortician												
patho-logist												
union organizer												

© 2005 The Critical Thinking Co. • www.CriticalThinking.com • 800-458-4849

10. Old Cars

Four married couples (Edgewoods, Framptons, Learneds, and MacArthurs) each have an old car (Hudson, Kaiser, Packard, and Studebaker) for the first time. The wives' first names are Anne, Cheryl, Jessica, and Nora. The husbands' first names are Bertram, Douglas, Gino, and Rex.

Match up everything from the clues below.

(Note: Read carefully. If a clue says something like, "John and Mary talked about their car," then you have two people and one car, so John and Mary must be married. But if it says "cars" instead of "car," then John and Mary must not be married, since each couple have only one old car.)

1. The Edgewoods, who do not have the Kaiser, asked Nora how she found her old car.

2. Neither Jessica and her husband nor the Learneds have the Packard or the Studebaker.

3. Gino and his wife, who don't own the Hudson, asked Cheryl and her husband if they thought the MacArthurs and the owners of the Studebaker would like to join the four of them for dinner.

4. The Framptons went to a baseball game with Rex and Bertram and their wives.

5. Jessica and Douglas were discussing how much their cars are worth when the Hudson owners came along and suggested they all take their cars to an appraiser.

6. Gino and his wife are not the Framptons.

7. Bertram and his wife don't have the Kaiser.

© 2005 The Critical Thinking Co. • www.CriticalThinking.com • 800-458-4849

Chart for Problem 10

	Bertram	Douglas	Gino	Rex	Edgewood	Frampton	Learned	MacArthur	Hudson	Kaiser	Packard	Stude-baker
Anne												
Cheryl												
Jessica												
Nora												
Edgewood												
Frampton												
Learned												
MacArthur												
Hudson												
Kaiser												
Packard												
Stude-baker												

11. At the Dairy Bar

Ed, Fred, Hope, and Ina walked into a dairy bar and seated themselves at four empty stools in a row so that males and females alternated. (We'll call these stools # 1, # 2, # 3, and # 4, with # 1 being the leftmost stool, looking at the stools' backs.) Their last names are Stewart, Taylor, Underwood, and Valera, and they ordered a banana split, an ice cream cone, a milkshake, and a sundae.

Match up everything from the clues below.

1. Ed was seated between the two girls.

2. Ina sat on Stewart's immediate right.

3. Taylor, who was the second to order, sat two seats from the person who ordered the milkshake and next to the person who ordered the ice cream cone.

4. Underwood sat at the immediate left of Valera and at the immediate right of the person who ordered the sundae.

5. Ina was the last to order.

© 2005 The Critical Thinking Co. • www.CriticalThinking.com • 800-458-4849

Chart for Problem 11

	Stewart	Taylor	Under-wood	Valera	banana split	ice cream cone	milkshake	sundae	1	2	3	4
Ed												
Fred												
Hope												
Ina												
banana split												
ice cream cone												
milkshake												
sundae												
1												
2												
3												
4												

© 2005 The Critical Thinking Co. • www.CriticalThinking.com • 800-458-4849

12. How Much Weight?

Adler, Durwood, Ericson, Farley, Gladstone, and Hamble, whose first names are Bernice, Christine, Melissa, Nicholas, Peter, and Stuart, want to lose weight. Each one wants to lose a different amount than the others, and the least amount is 5 kilograms.

From the clues below, figure out the amount of weight each person wants to lose, write this in on the chart, and then match this with the first and last names of the person.

1. Bernice is to lose 5 kilograms more than Adler but 5 kilograms less than Stuart.

2. Durwood must lose 5 kilograms more than Christine but 2 kilograms less than Gladstone.

3. Melissa is to lose 2 kilograms more than Nicholas but 3 kilograms less than Farley.

4. Peter must lose 2 kilograms less than Stuart and 3 kilograms more than Farley.

5. Christine is not Hamble.

© 2005 The Critical Thinking Co. • www.CriticalThinking.com • 800-458-4849

Chart for Problem 12

	Adler	Durwood	Ericson	Farley	Gladstone	Hamble	5 kg					
Bernice												
Christine												
Melissa												
Nicholas												
Peter												
Stuart												
5 kg												

© 2005 The Critical Thinking Co. • www.CriticalThinking.com • 800-458-4849

13. Drug Store Shopping

Adam, Dale, Ginger, and Jason, whose last names are Edgmont, Harper, Landon, and Morris, each bought something (cotton, newspaper, paperback book, and sunglasses) at a drug store (Olson's Drug Store, Reliable Drug Store, Taylor City Drug Store, and Vitamin Drugs). Just as each one left, he or she remembered something else needed (boric acid, fingernail file, hand lotion, and iodine) and went back and bought it too.

From the clues below, match up everything.

1. Dale, who didn't buy a paperback book or cotton, was glad she remembered the second item, which wasn't hand lotion, before she'd walked all the way back home.

2. On his way to the drug store, which wasn't Vitamin Drugs or Olson's, Harper saw Adam, who was just going home.

3. Morris saved gas by riding her bicycle to the drug store and back.

4. The person who bought the hand lotion didn't buy anything to read, and neither did Harper.

5. Neither the person who bought the cotton nor Edgmont bought boric acid or went to Reliable Drug Store.

6. The person who bought iodine at Olson's was neither Landon nor Adam.

© 2005 The Critical Thinking Co. • www.CriticalThinking.com • 800-458-4849

Chart for Problem 13

	Edgmont	Harper	Landon	Morris	Olson's	Reliable	Taylor City	Vitamin	cotton	newspaper	paperback	sunglasses	boric acid	fingernail file	hand lotion	iodine
Adam																
Dale																
Ginger																
Jason																
Olson's																
Reliable																
Taylor City																
Vitamin																
cotton																
newspaper																
paperback																
sunglasses																
boric acid																
fingernail file																
hand lotion																
iodine																

14. Domestic Flights

Akers, Bradley, Capper, and Darby, whose first names are Greta, Harry, Isabel, and Joseph, all flew from one city to another yesterday afternoon. All flights were primarily east to west or west to east, rather than north to south or south to north.

The cities left were Chicago, Minneapolis, San Francisco, and Washington, D.C. The cities arrived at were Detroit, New York City, St. Louis, and Tacoma. The times the flights left were 2:45, 3:10, 3:45, and 4:15 in their respective standard time zones.

Match up everything from the clues below.

1. The flight to St. Louis left at a later time than the flight from San Francisco but at an earlier time than the flight to New York City.

2. Akers' flight, unlike Isabel's, was from east to west.

3. Darby's flight, which left at a later time than the flight to New York City left, was shorter than Harry's flight but longer than the flight from Chicago.

4. Converting all departure times to eastern standard time, Capper's flight left the latest.

5. Joseph did not go to Tacoma.

© 2005 The Critical Thinking Co. • www.CriticalThinking.com • 800-458-4849

Chart for Problem 14

	Akers	Bradley	Capper	Darby	Chicago	Minneapolis	San Francisco	Washington, D.C.	Detroit	New York	St. Louis	Tacoma	2:45	3:10	3:45	4:15
Greta																
Harry																
Isabel																
Joseph																
Chicago																
Minneapolis																
San Francisco																
Washington, DC																
Detroit																
New York																
St. Louis																
Tacoma																
2:45																
3:10																
3:45																
4:15																

© 2005 The Critical Thinking Co. • www.CriticalThinking.com • 800-458-4849

SOLUTIONS

GENERAL COMMENTS ABOUT SOLUTIONS

There is more than one way to approach the solution of most Mind Benders®. For example, if a problem has five clues, you might choose to apply clue 4 first and clue 2 second, while the solution given for that problem uses clue 3 first and clue 5 second. Since there is only one final answer to the problem, the order in which the clues are used does not affect the final answer.

In order to understand a given solution, it is necessary that you have a copy of the problem to refer to while you are reading the solution. Also, it is definitely suggested, particularly for the problems in the B and C series, that you write down the findings as you go through a solution in order to help keep track of the rationale. For example, suppose a problem uses first and last names and occupations of three people. Before you start reading the solution here, write down the first names, leaving space to fill in the last names and occupations:

    Bernard

    Catherine

    Donald

This is what your notes will look like as you read through (part of) the detailed solution, "Smith is a man (2) but isn't Donald (4), so he is Bernard."

    Bernard Smith

    Catherine

    Donald

"The TV repairer is a man (3) but isn't Smith (3), so he is Donald."

    Bernard Smith

    Catherine

    Donald   TV repairer

Notice in the above example that clue numbers are referred to in parentheses.

© 2005 The Critical Thinking Co. • www.CriticalThinking.com • 800-458-4849

DETAILED SOLUTIONS

1.

NAME	GAME
Charles Darby	red rover
Edward Frye	hide and seek
Irene Wilson	Simon says
José Bingman	red light
Patricia Morgan	tag

Patricia likes "red rover" (2), a running game, so Patricia isn't Wilson (5). Wilson is a female (5), and so is Morgan (3), so Patricia is Morgan, and Irene is Wilson, whose favorite game is "Simon says" (5, the only game which doesn't have to involve running). Charles is not Frye (4) or Bingman (5), so Charles is Darby. José is not Frye (3), so he is Bingman, and Edward is Frye.

Patricia's favorite game is not "hide and seek" (1, male), "red rover" (2) or "red light" (4, male), so her favorite game is "tag." Charles Darby's favorite game is not "red light" (4), or "hide and seek" (1), so his favorite game is "red rover." "Red light" is not Frye's favorite game (4), so it is Bingman's, and Frye's favorite is "hide and seek."

2.

NAME	ICE CREAM FLAVOR
Elmer Hinton	strawberry
Frank Anderson	vanilla
Michelle Jones	chocolate
Nerissa Dowden	butter pecan
Zora Garvey	lemon

Zora is female (6). Hinton (1) and Anderson (2) are males. Elmer isn't Anderson (3), so Frank is, and Elmer is Hinton.

The girl whose favorite is butter pecan (3) isn't Michelle (3) or Zora (6), so she is Nerissa. Nerissa isn't Jones (1, butter pecan) or Garvey (3, butter pecan), so she is Dowden. Michelle is not Garvey (3), so she is Jones, and Zora is Garvey.

The girl whose favorite is lemon (4) is not Michelle (4), so she is Zora. Strawberry is not the favorite of Anderson (5) or Jones (5, Michelle), so it is the favorite of Hinton. Anderson's favorite is not chocolate (2), so it is vanilla, and Jones' favorite is chocolate.

3.

NAME	COLOR	CAT
Abner Magland	yellow	Pretty
Crystal Harmon	black	Kitty
Edmund Dinton	white	Sleepy
Joy Landon	gray	Fluffy

Magland has the yellow cat (1). Crystal doesn't have the yellow cat (5), so she is not Magland. Also, she isn't Landon or Dinton (3), so she is Harmon. Abner isn't Landon or Dinton (3), so he is Magland.

Two of the cats are short-haired, and the other two are long-haired (3), so Edmund owns a long-haired cat (4). Then he is Dinton (3), and so Joy is Landon.

Abner Magland's yellow cat is short-haired (3), so it is Pretty (4). Then Landon owns the gray cat (3, 4). Crystal doesn't have the white cat, so Edmund has it, and Crystal's cat is black.

Sleepy is not owned by Joy or Crystal Harmon (2), so Sleepy is Edmund's cat. Crystal doesn't own Fluffy (5), so she owns Kitty, and Joy owns Fluffy.

4.

NAME	FAMILY MEMBER
Caroline Newton	father
Dominic Reisner	mother
Edna Zaharias	brother
Gary Kaufman	sister
Helmut O'Brien	aunt
Inez Wyndham	uncle

No male caught a cold from a male (8). Neither Edna (4) nor Caroline (6) caught her cold from an uncle, so Inez did. Edna didn't catch a cold from her father (4), so she caught her cold from a brother, and Caroline caught her cold from her father.

The males are Kaufman and O'Brien (3) and Reisner (2). O'Brien is not Gary (5) or Dominic (7), so he is Helmut. Neither Gary nor Helmut O'Brien caught a cold from a mother (5), so Dominic did. Helmut didn't catch his cold from a sister (2), so he caught it from an aunt, and Gary caught his from a sister. Then Gary is not Reisner (2, sister), so he is Kaufman, and Dominic is Reisner.

Caroline is not Zaharias (6), and neither is Inez (6, uncle), so Edna is Zaharias. Caroline is not Wyndham (1), so Inez is, and Caroline is Newton.

© 2005 The Critical Thinking Co. • www.CriticalThinking.com • 800-458-4849

5.

NAME	HOW COOLED
Ada Ipson	department store
George Cranbrook	hose spray
Joanne Kribb	fan
Myrtle Emmerson	basement
Nehemiah Larson	swimming

Joanne used a fan (1). The person who sat under a hose spray was not Ipson or Larson (3) or Emmerson (2) or Kribb (4), so he or she was Cranbrook.

The person who went swimming was not Ada (2) or George or Myrtle (5), so he was Nehemiah. Cranbrook is a male (4, hose spray) but isn't Nehemiah (swimming), so Cranbrook is George.

The person who stayed in the basement was not Ipson or Larson (3) or Kribb (6), so she or he was Emmerson. Then Emmerson is not Joanne (fan), Nehemiah (swimming), or Ada (2), so Emmerson is Myrtle. Then Ada spent the afternoon at a department store. Then Ada is not Kribb (6) or Larson (7), so Ada is Ipson. Ada Ipson knows Joanne (1) but doesn't know Larson (7), so Joanne is not Larson. Then Nehemiah is Larson, and Joanne is Kribb.

6.

NAME	BREAD	MARMALADE
Amelia Johnstone	rye	strawberry
Bernard Ingles	pumpernickel	raspberry
Derick Horton	whole wheat	cherry
Eula May Grader	French bread	orange

Bernard is the youngest (6), so his marmalade is not orange (2) or cherry (4). It is not strawberry (6), so it is raspberry.

The whole wheat bread eater is one of the two youngest (2), but Amelia is one of the two oldest (4), so Amelia didn't eat the whole wheat bread. She also didn't eat the French bread (5) or the pumpernickel (4), so she ate the rye bread.

Horton is a male (3) but isn't Bernard (3), so he is Derick. Johnstone, who is not the youngest (2), is not Bernard (6, youngest) or Eula May (7), so she is Amelia.

Johnstone is not the oldest or the youngest (2) and is not the second youngest (4, Amelia), so she is the second oldest. Then Derick Horton, who is not the oldest or the youngest (1), is the second youngest, which makes Ingles the youngest (1), so Ingles is Bernard (6). Then Grader is Eula May.

Amelia didn't have cherry (4) or orange (5) marmalade, so she had strawberry. The person who had orange marmalade is older than Johnstone (2), who is second oldest, so this person is the oldest. Then this person is not Horton (second youngest), so she is Grader. Then Horton had cherry marmalade.

The person who had pumpernickel is one of the two youngest (4), and so this person is Bernard or Derick. He isn't Derick (4, cherry marmalade), so he is Bernard. The person who had orange marmalade (Grader) didn't have whole wheat bread (2), so Horton did, and Grader had French bread.

7.

NAME	PET	COLLAR
Allan Kingsley	zebra	green
Daphne Franklin	buffalo	yellow
Eunice Lohmer	cheetah	red
Howard Jackson	vulture	white

The buffalo has a yellow collar (1). The red collar is not worn by the vulture (5) or the zebra (6), so the cheetah wears it.

The vulture isn't the pet of Allan (5), Daphne (4), or Eunice (3), so it is Howard's pet. Its collar isn't green (2), so it is white. Then the zebra's collar is green. The cheetah isn't Allan's (5, red collar) or Daphne's (4), so it is Eunice's. Eunice isn't Franklin (3), Jackson (6), or Kingsley (4, cheetah), so she is Lohmer. Howard, who has the vulture, isn't Franklin (3) or Kingsley (4), so he is Jackson. Daphne isn't Kingsley (4), so Allan is, and Daphne is Franklin.

Franklin's pet is not the zebra (3, green collar), so it is the buffalo, and so Kingsley has the zebra.

8.

NAME	FACE	STYLE	ITEMS
Adam Grady	Korinna	extra bold	stationery
Deborah Ralston	Futura	medium	purchase orders
Joan Nelson	Oracle	bold	invoices
Vladimir Tyler	Helios	light	circulars

Nelson is a woman (2) but is not Deborah (2), so she is Joan. Then Ralston, also a woman (1), is Deborah. Adam isn't Tyler (1), so Vladimir is, and Adam is Grady.

The person who ordered Futura typeface is female (4) but isn't Nelson (2), so she is Ralston.

The invoices were not ordered by Grady (1, Adam) or by Tyler or Ralston (1), so Nelson ordered them. The type style wasn't medium (1) or light or extra bold (2), so it was bold. The typeface wasn't Helios (1) or Korinna (2), so it was Oracle.

Ralston didn't order light or extra bold type style (4, Futura), so she ordered medium type style.

© 2005 The Critical Thinking Co. • www.CriticalThinking.com • 800-458-4849

Neither Grady nor Ralston ordered the circulars (3), so Tyler ordered them. They were not printed in extra bold type style (3), so they were printed in light type style. Then Grady's items were printed in extra bold type style.

Ralston didn't order stationery (4, Futura), so Grady ordered it, and Ralston ordered purchase orders. Grady didn't order Helios typeface (5, extra bold), so he ordered Korinna, and Tyler ordered Helios.

9.

NAME	OCCUPATION
Arthur Stoker	mortician
Bartholemew O'Rourke	cosmetologist
Deborah Keyser	pathologist
Edith Werner	hair stylist
Francesca Tyler	labor arbitrator
Gordon Jankowski	union organizer

Keyser, a female (1) who is the pathologist (1), is not Francesca or Edith (7), so she is Deborah. Werner (4) and Tyler (5) are females, but Edith isn't Tyler (5), so she is Werner, and Francesca is Tyler.

Arthur is not O'Rourke (3) or Jankowski (5), so he is Stoker. Gordon is not O'Rourke (6), so Bartholemew is, and Gordon is Jankowski.

From clue 5, the cosmetologist is not Edith, Francesca (Tyler), Arthur, or Gordon (Jankowski), so Bartholemew is the cosmetologist. Since neither a labor arbitrator nor a union organizer has to know how to style hair, Stoker is neither of these (2), and he is not the hair stylist (2). So he is the mortician.

Neither Francesca nor Edith is the union organizer (7), so Gordon is.

Although a cosmetologist needs to be tactful, it is not realistic to say that part of the job is doing what a labor arbitrator does, so Werner is not the labor arbitrator (4, since Bartholemew is the cosmetologist). Then Tyler is the labor arbitrator, and Werner is the hair stylist.

10.

Jessica doesn't own the Packard or the Studebaker (2) or the Hudson (5), so she owns the Kaiser.

Frampton isn't Bertram or Rex (4) or Gino (6), so he is Douglas. Then Jessica is not

WIFE	HUSBAND	CAR
Anne Edgewood	Gino	Packard
Cheryl Learned	Bertram	Hudson
Jessica MacArthur	Rex	Kaiser
Nora Frampton	Douglas	Studebaker

Frampton (5, Douglas) or Learned (2) or Edgewood (1, Kaiser), so she is MacArthur.

The Learneds don't own the Packard or the Studebaker (2), so they own the Hudson. Gino is not Learned (3, Hudson) or MacArthur (3), so he is Edgewood.

Jessica MacArthur is not married to Bertram (7, Kaiser), so she is married to Rex. Then Bertram is Learned.

Gino doesn't have the Studebaker (3), so Douglas has it, and Gino has the Packard.

Cheryl isn't married to Gino (3) or to Douglas (3, Studebaker), so she is married to Bertram. Nora isn't married to Gino (1, Edgewood), so Anne is, and Nora is married to Douglas.

11.

The information in the first paragraph of the problem will be referred to below as "*".

NAME	TREAT	STOOL
Ed Valera	ice cream cone	3
Fred Stewart	sundae	1
Hope Taylor	banana split	4
Ina Underwood	milkshake	2

Ina is not Stewart (2) or Taylor (3, 5). Ina has Stewart on her immediate left (2), so she is not Valera (4). Then Ina is Underwood. She has Stewart on her left (2) and Valera on her right (4), so Stewart and Valera are males (*). Then Hope is Taylor.

The person who sat two seats away from Hope is Ina (*), so Ina ordered the milkshake (3). Males and females alternated in the seating arrangement (*), so Valera (4), Stewart (2), the person who ordered the sundae (4), and the person who ordered the ice cream cone (3) are males. Valera didn't order the sundae (4), so Stewart did, and so Valera ordered the ice cream cone. This leaves Taylor to order the banana split.

Combining what we have with clue 4, we have a partial seating arrangement:

Stewart (sundae), Ina Underwood (milkshake), Valera (ice cream cone).

Then clue 3 says that Taylor was on stool no. 4. Since Ed was between the two females (1), he is Valera. Then Fred is Stewart.

12.

NAME	WEIGHT TO LOSE
Bernice Farley	10 kg
Christine Ericson	8 kg
Melissa Hamble	7 kg
Nicholas Adler	5 kg
Peter Durwood	13 kg
Stuart Gladstone	15 kg

Combining clues 3 and 4, we have a partial ranking of the weight to be lost:

Nicholas $<^{+2}$ Melissa $<^{+3}$ Farley $<^{+3}$ Peter $<^{+2}$ Stuart.

This says Farley has 5 kilograms less to lose than Stuart, so Bernice is Farley (1). Similarly, Adler is Nicholas (1). So we now have Nicholas Adler $<^{+2}$ Melissa $<^{+3}$ Bernice Farley $<^{+3}$ Peter $<^{+2}$ Stuart.

Applying clue 2 to this listing, we see that Durwood isn't Stuart (since Christine can't be listed in the same place as Bernice). If Melissa is Durwood, then Christine would fall before Nicholas in the list (2), thus accounting for all six people, and yet Gladstone would have to fall between Melissa and Bernice (2), a contradiction. So Melissa isn't Durwood. Christine isn't Durwood (2), so Peter is Durwood. Then Stuart is Gladstone (2). Christine isn't Hamble (5), so Melissa is, and Christine is Ericson. Christine is to lose 5 kilograms less than Peter Durwood (2), so she falls between Melissa and Bernice in the list:

Nicholas Adler $<^{+2}$ Melissa Hamble $<^{+1}$ Christine Ericson $<^{+2}$ Bernice Farley $<^{+3}$ Peter Durwood $<^{+2}$ Stuart Gladstone.

Since we now have all six people listed, and since 5 kilograms is the least amount, we have the final result shown in the chart above.

13.

NAME	STORE	ITEM 1	ITEM 2
Adam Edgmont	Vitamin	sunglasses	hand lotion
Dale Landon	Reliable	newspaper	boric acid
Ginger Morris	Olson's	paperback book	iodine
Jason Harper	Taylor City	cotton	fingernail file

Dale is a woman (1). Morris is a woman who rode her bicycle to the drug store and back (3), so Morris isn't Dale (1, walked). Then Morris is Ginger. Harper is a man (2) but isn't Adam (2), so Harper is Jason. Adam isn't Landon (6), so he is Edgmont, and Dale is Landon.

The person who bought iodine at Olson's wasn't Landon or Adam Edgmont (6) or Harper (2), so this person was Ginger Morris. The person who bought hand lotion wasn't Dale Landon (1) or Harper (4), so Edgmont bought hand lotion.

A paperback book wasn't bought by Dale Landon (1) or Harper (4) or Edgmont (4, hand lotion), so Morris bought a paperback book.

Neither Dale Landon (1) nor Adam Edgmont (5) bought cotton, so Jason Harper bought it. Then neither Jason Harper nor Edgmont went to Reliable Drug Store (5), so Dale Landon went there. Harper didn't go to Vitamin Drugs (2), so Edgmont went there, and Harper went to Taylor City Drug Store.

Harper (5, cotton) didn't buy boric acid, so Landon bought it, and Harper bought a fingernail file. Edgmont didn't buy a newspaper (4, hand lotion), so Landon bought it, and Edgmont bought sunglasses.

14.

NAME	FROM	TO	DEPARTURE TIME
Greta Darby	Minneapolis	Tacoma	4:15
Harry Capper	San Francisco	Detroit	2:45
Isabel Bradley	Chicago	New York City	3:45
Joseph Akers	Washington, D.C.	St. Louis	3:10

The information in the problem's opening paragraph will be referred to below as "*".

From clue 1 and the first part of clue 3, we may list the order in which the flights departed:

from San Francisco, to St. Louis, to New York City, Darby.

Pairing this list with the list of departure times given, we have

from San Francisco, 2:45
to St. Louis, 3:10
to New York City, 3:45
Darby, 4:15

San Francisco is three hours behind eastern standard time. Chicago and Minneapolis are one hour behind eastern standard time, and Washington, D.C. is on eastern standard time. Converting all departure times to eastern standard time, we have

from San Francisco, 5:45
to St. Louis, 3:10 or 4:10
to New York City, 3:45 or 4:45
Darby, 4:15 or 5:15

Then Capper took the flight from San Francisco (4). Capper didn't go to St. Louis or New York City (schedule above) or to Tacoma (*), so he or she went to Detroit. Darby didn't go to St. Louis or New York City (schedule above), so she or he went to Tacoma. Akers went from east to west (2), so Akers didn't go to New York City.

© 2005 The Critical Thinking Co. • www.CriticalThinking.com • 800-458-4849

Then Akers went to St. Louis, and Bradley went to New York City.

If Darby, who flew to Tacoma, had left from Washington, D.C., then this flight time would have been the longest of all four. But it wasn't the longest (3), so Darby didn't leave from Washington, D.C. Darby didn't leave from Chicago (3), so she or he left from Minneapolis. A flight from Chicago to St. Louis is primarily north-south, so Akers (to St. Louis) didn't leave from Chicago (*).

Then Akers left from Washington, D.C., and Bradley left from Chicago.

The only flight which would take longer than Darby's (Minneapolis to Tacoma) would be Capper's (San Francisco to Detroit), so Capper is Harry (3). Darby, who flew west to Tacoma, is not Isabel (2) or Joseph (5), so Darby is Greta. Isabel isn't Akers (2), so Joseph is, and Isabel is Bradley.

© 2005 The Critical Thinking Co. • www.CriticalThinking.com • 800-458-4849